Crime Reduction Research Series Paper 1

Burglary prevention:

Early lessons from the Crime Reduction Programme

Nick Tilley, Ken Pease, Mike Hough and Rick Brown

Editor: Barry Webb
Home Office
Policing and Reducing Crime Unit
Research, Development and Statistics Directorate
Clive House, Petty France
London, SW1H 9HD

RDS
Research Development Statistics

The Policing and Reducing Crime Unit (PRCU) is based in the Research, Development and Statistics (RDS) Directorate of the Home Office. The Unit carries out and commissions social and management science research on policing and crime reduction, to support Home Office aims and develop evidence-based policy and practice.

The Crime Reduction Research Series presents research findings and guidance material relevant to practitioners involved in crime reduction at the local level, and particularly the local crime and disorder partnerships. The series will include work funded under the Government's Crime Reduction Programme as well as other relevant RDS work.

Details of how to obtain further copies of this report can be found on the back cover.

Foreword

This report is the first in a series to be published on the Burglary Reduction Initiative, a major element of the government's Crime Reduction Programme. The Burglary Reduction Initiative is an evidence-based programme that aims to reduce burglary nationally by targeting high crime neighbourhoods.

The first phase of the Burglary Reduction Initiative involves a series of Strategic Development Projects (SDPs). These aim to provide a knowledge base for understanding which burglary reduction methods work in what circumstances and will be subject to extensive evaluation. Successful approaches to burglary reduction will then be rolled out in later stages of the programme.

A development visit was made to each of these SDPs by Home Office employed consultants. The purpose of these visits was to assist SDP teams to refine their projects by ensuring they fully understood the nature of their burglary problem and offering advice on how to tailor interventions relevant to the local problem. This report is based on the experiences of those undertaking these visits.

The report provides an account of the lessons learned from these development visits. It highlights the varied nature of local burglary problems, summarises the range of interventions employed and identifies some of the obstacles to developing effective burglary reduction projects.

GLORIA LAYCOCK
Policing and Reducing Crime Unit
Research, Development and Statistics Directorate
Home Office
August 1999

Acknowledgements

We would like to thank the several hundred people from local Crime and Disorder Partnerships we met during our visits to Strategic Development Projects, who are too numerous to name individually. We were invariably treated hospitably and with considerable tolerance at our, sometimes naïve sounding, questions. The findings in this report and our ability to offer recommendation for how burglary reduction projects might be improved in future are based largely on our discussions with these individuals.

The Authors

Nick Tilley is Professor of Sociology at Nottingham Trent University, currently on secondment to the Home Office Policing and Reducing Crime Unit. Ken Pease OBE is Professor of Criminology at Huddersfield University, currently on secondment to the Home Office Policing and Reducing Crime Unit. Michael Hough is Professor of Social Policy and Director of the Criminal Policy Research Unit at South Bank University. Rick Brown is Programme Director of the Burglary Reduction Initiative Evaluation in the Home Office Policing and Reducing Crime Unit.

PRCU would like to thank Marcus Felson, professor at Rutgers University School of Criminal Justice for acting as independent assessor for this report.

Executive Summary

This report is the first in a series to present the findings from the Burglary Reduction Initiative, a major element of the Crime Reduction Programme launched in 1998. The first phase of the Burglary Reduction Programme involved commissioning a series of Strategic Development Projects (SDPs) in high burglary communities and were designed to extend current knowledge of cost-effective burglary prevention measures. These SDPs will form the basis upon which future burglary reduction projects are designed.

In the early stages of developing these projects, the authors acted as Home Office appointed consultants, assisting local crime and disorder partnerships to refine their approaches to tackling their local burglary problem. This report provides the lessons learned from that exercise.

Identifying and understanding the local burglary problem

Local crime and disorder partnerships participating in the initiative were required to identify areas with a rate of domestic burglary twice the national average over three years and with between 3,000 and 5,000 households (areas with fewer households were permitted if the number of burglaries exceeded 100). This often proved difficult and some of the common problems encountered were:

- Aligning administrative boundaries so that burglary data, based on police areas, could be compared with household data, based on local authority areas, in order to produce rates of burglary.

- Identifying burglary problems that crossed administrative boundaries. For example, a high burglary rate might be found at the point where two police beats meet.

- Examining trends over time. Changes to IT systems and to administrative boundaries often made it difficult to examine burglary rates over a number of years.

One of the striking impressions gained from visiting the SDPs was the wide range of ways in which the varying elements of the 'chemistry of burglary' can be brought together. Appendix A provides some accounts drawn from these visits. Many factors contribute to local crime problems but can be categorised into five key types of crime generator – 1. offender related; 2. victim related; 3. community related; 4. specific situational and 5. wider locality related generators. Local burglary problems will often contain a combination of these factors and burglary reduction projects need to be tailored to take these into account.

During the course of the visits to SDPs, a number of local burglary problems emerged that had not previously been fully appreciated. Many of these were related to the role of privately rented accommodation. For example, students, who tend to live in cheap privately rented accommodation, suffered a high level of victimisation. Their typical age (young), income (low), tenure (privately rented), hours leaving property empty (many), accommodation type (flats and terraced houses) and employment status all put them at high risk. From the area perspective, the decline of some traditional seaside towns had led to an increase in bed and breakfast accommodation and flatlets rented to groups most at risk of engaging in burglary. In other areas, there had been a collapse in the local housing market, resulting in cheap houses being bought by landlords, who can make a quick return on their investment by renting to those on housing benefit, some of whom will be offenders, but all potential victims of burglary.

Devising solutions

Given the wide variety of burglary problems identified, it is unsurprising that these were matched by an equally varied range of interventions. In general, these aimed to tackle either offender related generators, victim related generators, specific situational generators, or wider locality related generators of crime. In most cases, the projects developed in the SDPs involved a package of interventions. In some cases, these involved interactive approaches in which one intervention was dependent on others (e.g. crack-down and consolidation in which enforcement is followed by community self-confidence building). Others could be classed as combined packages in which long lists of interventions were proposed but not necessarily integrated with each other. Finally some SDPs had planned contradictory approaches in which one intervention worked to the detriment of another (e.g. target hardening preventing the success of covert detection methods employing tracking devices).

SDPs and the bidding process

Much was learned about the process of allocating resources from the first round of the burglary reduction initiative that will be of benefit for future rounds of the programme:

Type of area eligible for funding: the difficulties in identifying geographic areas fitting the criteria, suggests there may be benefits from taking a more flexible approach to identifying burglary problems. This might also allow for 'virtual communities'[1] of victimised groups (e.g. students) who suffer from burglary but do not necessarily live in close proximity to each other.

Funding available: a ceiling of £60,000 per project was placed on funding for SDPs. Consideration should be given to funding projects on the basis of a formula related to the size of the burglary problem, or the number of households.

The initial bids: local areas varied in their familiarity with the process of preparing bids for government funding and this affected the quality of the bids received, although a well "polished" bid was not always a good indicator of the best projects. Target-setting for the expected reduction to be achieved was a particular problem as this was seldom based on rational calculations.

---

[1] By 'virtual community' we mean a community that is defined in terms of features other than a common geography.

The development visits: Those visited were not always clear what was expected of them. The extent to which proposals were developed also varied considerably from project to project. It was invariably helpful to visit the site of the proposed intervention and to talk about the area and its burglary problem with those who had first hand experience of working in the area.

The revised bids: In many cases, the revised bids were much more comprehensive than the original outline bids and showed that a great deal of thought had gone into them. In one or two cases, further analysis of the problem had resulted in little adjustment in the strategy.

Recommendations

The paper includes a number of recommendations on how burglary reduction efforts might be improved in future. These include recommendations related to planning local burglary reduction projects and highlights the need for a strategic approach that incorporates analysis of the local problem that provides the basis for generating sustainable crime reduction measures. There are also recommendations related to the future operation of the burglary reduction initiative, focusing on the criteria for selecting burglary problems, the timing for the preparation of plans and the method of funding projects. Finally, there are recommendations for how burglary problems could be addressed centrally, by reducing the vulnerability of students, designing crime prevention features in products most commonly targeted in burglaries and promoting campaigns that reduce the acceptability of buying stolen goods.

Contents

List of tables

1.   Introduction

In mid 1998 the Government announced a £250 million crime reduction programme (CRP), a prominent part of which involved residential burglary. In November 1998 the Home Office invited police forces and local authorities to bid to fund burglary prevention projects. In the course of assessing the bids the authors of this report visited all the bidding sites, which included many of the worst burglary hotspots in the country. We discussed the nature of burglary problems with police and council officials who had detailed local knowledge; we examined the data they held about burglary; we discussed their plans for tackling the problem. In the course of this process, we felt that we learnt a great deal, not only about patterns of residential burglary in the late 1990s but also about emerging strategies for its control. We also got a sense of how the planning process was experienced at the local level. This report is an attempt to draw out some lessons from the experience.

The Crime Reduction Programme

The Crime Reduction Programme emerged from the Government's wide-ranging Comprehensive Spending Review (CSR) of 1998. The Home Office CSR incorporated an overview of approaches to crime reduction (Goldblatt and Lewis 1998). This informed the government's decision to allocate £250 million to a Crime Reduction Programme (CRP), set to run over three years in the first instance. The CRP realises the commitment to evidence-led policy. The CRP will allow scope for developing new approaches to crime reduction and for making refinements to existing practice. Underlying this is the need to identify what works most cost effectively in reducing crime in what circumstances and to this end, some 10% of the CRP's £250 million have been earmarked for evaluation research.

The Burglary Reduction Initiative

One strand of the CRP relates to domestic burglary, which remains a high volume crime, with attendant financial and emotional costs for its victims. It also results in significant public expenditure through the criminal justice system. The CRP therefore allocated a minimum of £50 million to schemes seeking to reduce domestic burglary, destined eventually to cover around two million households in high crime communities.

As a first step in the burglary reduction component of the CSR, local crime and disorder partnerships were invited to bid for funding as Strategic Development Projects (SDPs). They were asked to identify areas each comprising 3,000 - 5,000 households, which had experienced at least twice the national recorded domestic burglary rate for each of the previous three years. Smaller areas were also eligible for funding if they experienced at least 100 burglaries per year. They were also asked to sketch out briefly the main elements of their proposed strategy to reduce that rate and to suggest targets for the scale of the anticipated reduction. Bidders were told that successful areas were unlikely to receive more than £60,000, and that successful bidders should plan to spend the bulk of the money allocated within twelve months. Invitations to bid were sent out in November 1998 and outline bids were submitted to the Home Office by the beginning of 1999.

This process generated 125 bids, of which 60 were provisionally selected as SDPs and six were placed on a reserve list. Criteria for selection included the novelty of the proposed strategy, the context (type of problem, location etc.) in which established methods were to be applied and the quality of the available data and data systems[2].

One of the conditions of eligibility for funding as an SDP was agreement that partners would 'work in co-operation with Home Office appointed consultants to develop proposals for the cost-effective reduction of domestic burglary in the intervention area and to provide detailed costed implementation plans.' Indeed, the original bid document required that a 'Partnership Declaration' be signed by a police officer (Commander or above) and the local authority Chief Executive confirming this. The writers are those consultants. This first report of the Crime Reduction Programme is based on our visits to the sixty short-listed burglary reduction SDPs and to the six projects that were on the reserve list. We were accompanied by data auditors from the Home Office, who examined the available data systems. The findings from these audits are the subject of a separate report.

In due course, there will be detailed evaluations of those projects selected as SDPs. These will be conducted by regionally-based independent contractors, appointed by the Home Office. A further set of burglary reduction SDPs is planned later in the programme.

The shape of this report

Our purpose in writing of our experience to date is to try and tease out early lessons for the Home Office and for local areas intending to submit proposals later in the CRP, both in relation to their plans to reduce burglary specifically, and in relation to their formulation of strategies to reduce crime more generally. Section 2 summarises our thoughts about the nature of burglary concentration and the processes which produce it. Section 3 offers some observations about the emerging strategies for reducing residential burglary in areas where it presents a particularly acute problem. Section 4 discusses the bidding process. A final section draws some conclusions.

The following discussion is testimony to the openness and hard work of those seen during our visits to SDPs. Local project teams were almost invariably hospitable and patient in their discussions of their plans. Moreover, they were keen to pick up whatever they could (even from Home Office appointed consultants!) to help their most burglary-prone residents. By the end of our visits we had learned a great deal about high burglary areas up and down the country, about efforts to reduce them, and about the process of preparing bids for government support. Although the points we make often highlight shortcomings in what we encountered, it is

---

[2] The aim was to evaluate the projects thoroughly, and this would be impossible in sites with poor data systems.

important for readers to bear two points in mind. First, given their success in a competitive bidding round, the SDPs visited were among the best and most thought-through crime prevention initiatives that could be planned at short notice. Second, a great deal of what we say we discovered from those to whom we spoke. To that extent, we are simply their mouthpieces.

2. Identifying and understanding the local burglary problem

Identifying the local problem

Identifying residential areas that met the criteria for inclusion as an SDP (an area of 3,000 to 5,000 households with a rate of domestic burglary twice the national average over a three year period, or smaller areas with at least 100 burglaries per year) was by no means easy. In many cases, this involved a number of processes, including defining the boundaries of the target area, identifying how many burglaries had occurred in that area and calculating this as a rate per 1,000 households in that location. At each stage, various problems were identified in what might have been considered a straight forward task.

Identifying the target area

One of the first problems encountered by many partnerships was identifying an area with the right number of households and burglaries to meet the criteria set for a burglary reduction project. In most cases, there appear to have been some initial decisions made on where to look for the burglary problem, based on the local knowledge of partnership staff working on the ground. This approach seems to have been preferred to a more comprehensive, statistical search for burglary problems across all neighbourhoods. The advantage of this approach is that selection was based on local awareness of where burglary was blighting local communities. However, this is also a disadvantage because it runs the risk of missing areas that have a less conspicuous but also large burglary problem. Given the limited availability and even more limited use of automated, analytical tools for identifying burglary concentration, the approach taken is entirely defensible and probably inevitable, given the short time scale. However, it has clear limitations in extending the initiative to cover all areas with high rates of burglary.

Once a problem has been provisionally identified locally, this needs to be translated into analysis of the available data to see if the perceived problem is reflected in the data. This often raised the problem of selecting the appropriate geographical unit on which to plot the burglary and household figures. Some partnerships started with local authority data on households (often based on wards) and then fitted the available burglary data to it, while others started with burglary data (often based on police beats) which was matched to household information. Whichever approach was taken, the problem remained the same – matching data collected by two organisations using slightly different boundaries for their geographical units[3]. Areas with advanced Geographic Information Systems (GIS) were able to define areas much more flexibly. They were, in effect, able to search for those which met the Home Office criteria and were not dependent on pre-existing ways of carving up households and crimes. In addition, some had systems in place for checking the accuracy of the geographical assignment of incidents (which can easily mislead, see Farrell and Pease, 1993). The downside of this more sophisticated method of finding eligible areas is that boundaries could seem (or indeed be) quite arbitrary. This problem was further exacerbated where shared

---

[3] There was evidence that the recent Crime and Disorder Audits had spurred some local partnerships to begin the process of aligning their administrative boundaries to assist with the sharing of data in future.

geographical information was anonymised in accordance with the perceived requirements for Data Protection. This often resulted in crime maps without street definition, which meant the edges of areas were poorly defined.

The flexible geography made available by GIS systems is probably most sensibly coupled with common sense and site visits to see what sorts of boundaries encompass meaningful and manageable areas.

Burglaries in the target area

The original prospectus required evidence of a burglary problem over three years. However, changes to local computer systems during this time meant it was often difficult to obtain information for all three years. Similarly, changes to local boundaries – either wards or police beats – made it difficult to plot the number of burglaries occurring in the target area over time.

Another problem was the inclusion of commercial and other non-domestic burglaries into the figures. Although in most cases, the figures provided were purely based on domestic burglaries, in two cases it was evident that commercial burglaries had also been included, although when separated out, the domestic burglary problem was still twice the national average. This confusion was partly a result of the original prospectus issued by the Home Office, which did not specify clearly enough that domestic burglary was the focus of concern.

In one force, burglary 'allegations' (based on initial incident reports) were used as the basis for calculating the number of burglaries, rather than confirmed burglary records. Although this made relatively little difference to the statistics, it tends to slightly over-estimate the actual number of burglaries in a target area.

Another problem encountered in one force was the selection of the wrong target area. By entering the wrong code into the crime analysis system, the burglary data for the neighbouring area was extracted. This resulted in a burglary reduction project being proposed for an area that did not have a significant burglary problem. Prior to this discovery, the discussion with practitioners had provided a rational explanation for why the proposed target area (with few burglaries in reality) had a significant burglary problem. People make sense of any pattern put before them (see, for example, Garfinkel 1967). This can lead to confusion and embarrassment when the data are wrong. Practitioners at our meeting drew on what 'everyone knows' about burglary and about the area to make apparent sense of patterns that the area did not exhibit. This highlights three issues. First, data can mislead; it is important to check conclusions carefully, especially where significant decisions follow from analyses. Second, folk understanding cannot be taken at face value; it can and will be conjured up as required, but requires independent checks. Third, there are advantages in external audits of data analyses.

Households in the target area

Counting households posed its own set of problems. In most cases, the count was based on 1991 census data, which is obviously coming to the end of its useful life as a means of profiling an area. This was particularly evident on a number of local authority estates in the north of England, where failure to let properties (often because of their reputation for having a crime problem) had resulted in their demolition. In one area, a series of medium rise blocks of flats were demolished, partly due to the drug problems experienced there. On another local authority estate, a whole street had been demolished and grassed over, because the council could not find people to move there, even when cash incentives were offered. From the data audits conducted on site, it was not always clear whether the household figures had been revised following these major changes to the area. Some local partnerships resolved such problems by using up-to-date address data-sets, which reduced dependence on the 1991 census.

Wards, used by many as the basic area unit, do not always describe homogenous areas. In one city, which struggled to find an area meeting the criteria for eligibility, wards fan out from the centre of town. The inner areas within each ward evidently experience high burglary rates and the outer areas do not. They also comprise differing housing types and resident patterns. Contiguous inner parts of wards would evidently comprise relatively homogenous households with much higher burglary rates than are to be found in individual wards. Here, ward level analysis was conducted because of its convenience in calculating household and burglary figures, not because this was the level that necessarily made most sense in planning a burglary reduction initiative. Enumeration districts (that are smaller, sub-ward areas), or other more flexible approaches to defining area boundaries may provide a more suitable basis for doing so.

The original SDP prospectus issued by the Home Office emphasised selecting areas with between 3,000 and 5,000 households, although it also allowed for smaller areas with a significant burglary problem. Most of the bids received from local partnerships met the 3,000 households criterion. Further analysis of the target areas during the development visits revealed that they may have been selected on this basis, rather than because the whole area suffered from a burglary problem. Residential burglary was sometimes concentrated on a small part of the ward / beat. Inclusion of the wider area in the project had the effect of understating and misplacing the burglary problem. This may, depending on the intervention chosen, dilute the intensity of intervention available for the part of the target area with the most acute problem.

Double-checking data on target areas

A significant number of bids were found to contain arithmetic errors in calculating the rates of burglary, suggesting that checks are essential. The reason for stressing this point is not to seek to embarrass those who submitted bids. The fact that they met a very short deadline and had a range of ideas which they wished to implement excited our admiration. It is merely to point out that there does not yet exist a culture in which data are scrutinised carefully, and in respect of which challenge is anticipated.

Geographical and virtual communities[4]

The original SDP prospectus envisaged projects covering a geographical area with a certain number of households and in which all households are included in the intervention area. This will often be the easiest way to conceptualise burglary problems because local partnership computer systems will be most effective at extracting data on geographical units. It will often be a helpful approach because domestic burglary is so unevenly distributed geographically. However, it is not necessarily the best approach. During the course of the development visits, it became clear that some socio-demographic groups were particularly prone to burglary victimisation. For example, students and those living in multiple occupied dwellings were identified as being prone to burglary at a number of SDP sites. Such groups need not necessarily occupy a spatially distinct area, but may be spread across a number of wards / beats. If burglary reduction projects are to target successfully such 'virtual communities', it may be necessary to widen the eligibility criteria to avoid selections based purely on spatial definitions.

The local chemistry of burglary

Marcus Felson (1998) has suggested that crimes have their own 'chemistries', and that it is useful to understand them in working out prevention strategies. To understand a crime chemistry he suggests we:

1   Figure out who and what must be present and absent for a crime to occur
2   Find out what slice of space and time (setting) makes this likely
3   Determine how people move into and out of the setting when committing an offence.

To commit a domestic burglary successfully, a motivated and capable potential offender must find his or her way to an accessible dwelling within which he or she believes there to be prospects at the time of finding suitable (notably portable, high value, and anonymous) targets for theft. Furthermore, there must at the time of the offence be no-one present who has the ability to prevent the burglary from taking place, either by dissuading the prospective burglar, or by providing plausible guardianship of the potential target. Moreover, the goods stolen must either be of intrinsic value to the would-be burglar or the burglar must have access to a stolen goods market whereby the goods can be converted to utilities: normally cash or drugs.

Thus, high burglary areas are those which are readily accessible to, or with a high resident population of likely burglars, which have a plentiful supply of accessible dwellings containing goods suitable for theft, and within which there are periods when there are few people or insufficient security hardware capable of providing perceived effective guardianship. Where capitalising on burglary involves the disposal of goods, there must be a stolen goods market to which the burglar has access. Reducing the burglary rate involves removing one or more of the critical elements from the local burglary chemistry.

---

[4] By 'virtual communities' we mean communities that are defined in terms of features other than a common geography.

One of the most striking impressions gained from visiting a large number of high burglary areas is the wide range of ways in which the varying elements for the chemistry of burglary can be brought together. The Appendix provides some accounts drawn from visits to the SDPs, highlighting what are taken by practitioners to be some of the key generators of high burglary rates and showing how these can combine in different ways to produce varied burglary problems. The following list attempts to distil some of the key crime generators identified from the SDPs:

Offender related generators

- A network of inter-generational 'problem families' responsible for much crime and anti-social behaviour in an area.
- The 'one man crime wave' – individuals responsible for large numbers of burglaries in the area they live in.
- Youths growing up in an area, influenced by their older offending peers.
- Local residents with a drug dependency who burgle their neighbours to obtain the necessary funds to purchase drugs.
- Individuals at high risk of engaging in burglary moving into an area due to a supply of cheap rented accommodation.
- Offenders travelling into an area specifically to burgle because of its reputation for rich pickings.
- Offenders who travel into an area as part of their routine activities and burgle while they are there.

Victim related generators

- Groups (notably students) initially naïve about the risks of crime moving into a high crime neighbourhood with a supply of desirable items.
- Transient populations renting accommodation for short periods, where relative anonymity prevents informal social control between neighbours.
- Resident populations who are willing to purchase stolen property, sometimes to replace the items they have lost through burglary victimisation.

Community related generators

- Low levels of informal social control in the community, associated with low participation in community events, little social interaction between neighbours etc.
- High levels of unemployment, under-employment and economic deprivation, that lower resident expectations of success through conventional legitimate channels of income generation and provide a partial rationalisation for engaging in crime.

Specific situational generators

- Poorly designed estates that afford limited opportunity for natural surveillance and provide networks of alleyways for offenders to approach and exit burglary targets by.

- Terraced housing with back alleys, where natural surveillance is limited, especially once the offender has entered the back yard of a property.
- Houses in Multiple Occupation (HIMOs) with shared entrances where it is not unusual to see strangers and where poor quality locks provide easy access to individual living units.
- Poor quality security on doors and windows in general.
- Poor street lighting, reducing potential for natural surveillance at night.

Wider locality related generators

- Leisure facilities (such as shopping centres, sports grounds) that draw large numbers of males at peak age of offending into an area.
- Area sited close to known offender populations.
- Good public transport links into an area.

Theory and evidence

The accounts in the Appendix comprise plausible scenarios setting out how one or more of the key elements in the chemistry of burglary had become concentrated in each local area. They have, for the most part, not yet been tested, or have only been partially tested. This is in part because necessary data were unavailable or inaccessible, and partly because available data had not been analysed. Where possible, it is clearly sensible to draw together available evidence to develop and test theories making sense of high burglary rates, before developing plans to tackle the problem. Here we are not implying the need for large-scale research exercises, it simply means that assumptions and beliefs about the nature and causes of the local burglary problem should be tested with available data.

Problems with gathering evidence to test theories

There are many problems associated with gathering information to test local 'chemistry of burglary' theories. Locally available data that might be used have normally been collected for other operational purposes. Clearly much evidence is fallible. Recorded crime data depend on reporting practices by the public and recording practices by the police. We know that both are partial. They are also variable from location to location. In one area it appeared that black residents experienced half the rate of burglary experienced by the rest of the community. It is at least possible to speculate that this may have to do with variations in burglary reporting and recording practices, though we lack any evidence that this contributes to the explanation.

Data on victim addresses, victim attributes, mode of entry to property, search patterns, goods stolen, and exit routes may be available in principle in many areas. In practice, they depend on the completeness and accuracy of the crime report, and this is acknowledged often to be patchy. Data on how goods are disposed of are generally thin.

The clear-up rates for residential burglary, where known, were seldom much higher than 20%, and often less than 10%. The proportion of burglaries directly detected is, of course, smaller, since some will be TICs (offences taken into consideration in addition to the crime in relation to which there is direct and adequate evidence of the individual's involvement). What can only be speculated upon, on the basis of data which underpinned the bids, is the actual number of offenders responsible for the known offences in the area. This is not to say that such information is in principle inaccessible, simply that it fell outside that which was made available during our visits.

Theories, including those about the local crime chemistry, can never be proven. That does not mean, though, that data are irrelevant to testing those theories or to planning initiatives. The following examples show how analysis of the available data was important in challenging misconceptions, upon which some burglary reduction projects had initially been based:

- In one area a passageway running through the area had been deemed crucial to the burglary problem, because of the rear access it gave to adjacent houses. Mapping the burglaries and examining modes of entry revealed this to be a likely misconception, since dwellings contiguous to the passageway were not more victimised than others.

- In another area, drugs were deemed important and a scheme was planned to make provision for drug-taking offenders. Examination of the data on offenders revealed that a negligible number of candidates for treatment would be identified, and this group was known to be responsible for a vanishingly small proportion of all burglaries in the area. This is not to say that drugs were not important as a motive for burglary, simply that the group which was targeted for treatment did not contribute a major part of the problem.

Analysing the local chemistry of burglary

To gain an understanding of the local burglary problem, it probably makes sense routinely to attempt some standard analyses of the available data. Table 1 indicates the types of analysis that may be useful and some of the potential benefits accruing from these.

It will also be beneficial to take soundings from local residents, from housing officers, crime prevention officers, beat officers, patch-based scenes of crime officers, and local councillors to elicit ideas about what might explain the local burglary problems. In addition there is already a literature on domestic burglary and its prevention which can usefully be consulted (for example Bennett and Wright, 1984; Chenery et al, 1997; Davidson, 1984; Ekblom et al, 1996 ; Forrester et al, 1988, 1990; Anderson et al, 1995; Laycock, 1992; Pease, 1992; Polvi et al, 1990; Stockdale and Gresham, 1995; Tilley and Webb, 1994; Winchester and Jackson, 1982). Potential explanations of the local high burglary rate can then be assessed using the available data, with proper regard for their weaknesses.

One may have to act on untested assumptions, but checking the validity of those assumptions should be a priority. Effort could usefully be expended in working out what would be the

Table 1: *Types of analyses helpful for understanding the local chemistry of burglary*

Type of analysis	Benefit of analysis
Attributes of the property, (e.g. tenure type, dwelling type	Assists in identifying types of properties preferred by burglars. Helpful for understanding why such properties are targeted and for developing effective situational prevention measures.
Attributes of the victims (e.g. age, ethnicity, household composition)	Assists in identifying groups particularly prone to burglary and for whom a tailored burglary reduction package could be produced.
Geographical distribution of offences within the high burglary area. Point data is preferable to street or post-coded data.	Assists in identifying particular burglary hotspots. Also useful for showing changes in location of burglary over time (e.g. is hotspot temporary or more permanent?).
Patterns in the method by which burglaries are committed.	Assists in linking burglaries to the MOs of known offenders. Assists in identifying method of entry to properties that may help in targeting preventative action.
Patterns of repeat victimisation, including prevalence (no. of victims), incidence (no. of offences), concentration (no. of offences per victim) and rate (no. victimised once, twice, three times etc). A rolling year is more revealing than aggregations over a twelve month period.	Shows how burglary is distributed between households. Will help to identify locations / households suffering high burglary rate.
Profile of the known offenders.	Assists in identifying who is committing burglaries. Will enable assessments of whether the problem is endemic to the area, or imported and will inform approaches to targeting offenders.
Property stolen, and methods of disposal.	Assists in identifying any trends in types of goods stolen and will inform market reduction approaches to tackling the problem.
Ratio of successful to attempted burglaries.	Analysis of unsuccessful burglaries may give useful pointers to prevention. Tracking trends in attempts may provide insights into the impact of preventive measures.
Temporal patterns to burglary (e.g. time of day, day week, time of year).	Assists in identifying the key times when intervention may be most needed.

measurable implications of a particular assertion. For example, if burglary is supposed to be facilitated by the existence of back alleys, is rear entry more frequent than front entry?; when stolen goods are found nearby, does this suggest a rear exit?; is the burglary rate higher where there are back alleys?; when people erect their own gates to bar entry, does this confer any protection from burglary on the houses closest to the gate? If we can bring analytic and other resources to bear on the problem, the nature and distribution of burglaries will act as a signature to its causes.

Because little information was available on patterns of travel to and from burglary sites, use of motor vehicles, methods of selecting the target, co-offending patterns, methods of disposing of stolen goods, use of the money made through the burglary etc, in at least one area there are tentative plans to interrogate in more detail those asking for offences to be taken into consideration. More detailed interviewing could be used both to corroborate the admission to the offence and to collect information of potential use in preventing further crimes. It could, for example, generate information on those to whom stolen goods are being sold, how many offenders are known to be operating in an area, and so on. Examining the extent of co-offending is particularly important as this may provide a means of tackling local offender networks (see Reiss, 1988). In this regard, those who recruit young people into burglary (Reiss and Farrington, 1991) would merit particular attention, as these may account for the high prevalence of burglary offenders in some areas.

We were surprised to find that in some areas rather little had been done to think through the way local burglary problems were generated, or to consider the views of those with local experience of dealing with victims. At worst, received views were confidently asserted, with no apparent effort to make checks even when they were possible.

Emerging shapes of burglary problems

Some features of high burglary rate areas emerged, we think, more strongly than they have previously. However, we must stress an earlier point that these were areas which were locally identified as having problems, which may not be representative of areas suffering them.

In many SDPs, areas with large proportions of privately rented property emerged as often having burglary problems. Within these, HIMOs often figured as significant problems. Cases two, four and five in the Appendix provide examples. There appear both to be a number of generic problems with privately rented housing and with HIMOs in particular that contribute towards the burglary problem.

One generic problem concerns the frequently weak peripheral security of privately-rented houses, and especially of HIMOs. Those best placed to improve it are the landlords. Yet the landlords do not stand to benefit from expenditure on security. It is their tenants who suffer the losses. A second generic problem relates to internal security in HIMOs. Internal doors are often weak and easily breached once the house has been entered. Again landlords are best placed to make improvements but have little financial interest in paying for them. A third generic problem concerns the security behaviour of residents. Even where exterior doors are adequate, their potential in keeping intruders out often depends on residents making use of the devices fitted. They evidently often fail to do so. Moreover landlords may be reluctant to supply any other than cheap and easily replaced keys to tenants, who may be apt to lose them or to fail to return them. A final generic problem relates to fire regulations, which stress the need for easy and quick egress from buildings, which was seen by some to militate against the fitment of hard-to-penetrate peripheral security.

There would also appear to be a number of specific problems associated with the nature of tenants residing in private rented properties, which have not previously been fully appreciated:

- **Students as victims:** There are specific problems for students in the private rented sector. The 1998 BCS (Mirrlees-Black et al 1998) shows the risk factors for burglary. It looks at seven features of households: age of head, household composition, employment status, income, tenure, accommodation type, and hours unoccupied during the average weekday. Students are likely to be among the most at risk of burglary in almost all categories. Their typical age (young), income (low), tenure (privately rented), hours leaving property empty (many), accommodation type (flats and terraced houses) and employment status all put them at high risk. Moreover, they tend to live in poorer and cheaper parts of cities, where there may be higher prevailing crime rates, even before their own contribution as victims. They tend to arrive at college or university with a supply of the most popular goods taken in burglaries (readily portable, high value electronic equipment) and little local street wisdom. Cases two and four in the Appendix are examples. It should be no surprise that students experience high rates of burglary.

- **The decline of the seaside town:** Seaside towns also produce emerging burglary problems in HIMOs. Changing holiday patterns mean that traditional resorts are suffering economic decline. The tourist industry in them no longer thrives. Many houses are being turned over to bed and breakfast accommodation or are being converted into flatlets. A proportion of the unemployed new residents are attracted to the pleasant surroundings. Some are offenders. Many are thought to be dependent on illegal drugs. Burglars find simple opportunities among the residents in insecure HIMOs. Case 5 in the Appendix is just one example.

- **The collapse of local property markets:** Where there is an over-supply of housing, especially in parts of the North East and North West, demand for the least attractive private housing slumps; prices fall but prospective owner occupiers are deterred by the prospect of further falls. Such areas are quickly bought up by commercial landlords, who can get a rapid return on their investment by renting to people in receipt of housing benefit. This process can turn into a spiral of rapid decline, in which a potent burglary chemistry is generated. This brings together motivated offenders and targets lacking appropriate guardianship; high crime rates result.

- **Pushing problem families into the private rented sector:** The spiral of decline experienced by some areas is being exacerbated in some cases by strategies developed by partnerships between the police and local authorities designed to address problems of anti-social families and households living in local authority estates. Tenancy agreements are being more stringently enforced, sometimes supported by evidence provided by the police. When criminal families are dislodged through eviction from local authority housing, they are likely to end up in the privately rented sector as tenants of the least discriminating landlords. And when they resume their offensive and offending behaviour, they are likely to focus their attention on their immediate neighbours, further accelerating the spiral of decline.

- **Unanticipated consequences of local authority decisions:** There is some evidence that the existence or persistence of local burglary problems is a by-product of decisions taken for other policy reasons. In one case, the consequence of a decision not to approve the relocation of the (second division) football club away from the high burglary residential area, is that a large number of those most likely to commit burglary (young men) continue routinely to be brought into the area, where they can learn of the (plentiful) opportunities to commit burglary.

Persisting burglary problems

The SDPs reveal also that old sources of burglary continue:

- **Radburn estates:** The Radburn lay-out of housing estates is characterised by groups of dwellings approached by networks of footpaths and separated by grassed areas, often with communal car parking areas nearby. There is some evidence to suggest this type of estate continues to yield its burglary harvest. Cases one and three furnish examples, where lack of natural surveillance, ease of entry and ease of escape all seem to contribute to the high burglary rates. Case one is shocking for its recency of construction, and for the lack of foresight at the time in concentrating large numbers of young children in the same place, alongside what is known to be a vulnerable population.

- **Neighbourhoods with rookeries:** There continue to be areas of housing with well-established networks of criminal families associated with the commission of large numbers of burglaries. Case three in the Appendix provides an example. While many of these areas have, in recent decades, tended to be council estates, there is the possibility, as discussed above, that the problem could be displaced to the private rented sector.

● **Drug culture:** Many crime and disorder partnerships blamed their local burglary problem on a pervasive drug culture in the target area. This involved either a resident population of drug users who burgled neighbours to obtain the money they required, or a local drug market that attracted offenders into the area to burgle and buy drugs.

3.   Devising solutions

The discussion so far has stressed the need to understand how the elements in the chemistry for burglary are brought together to generate high rates in local areas. It has also shown how those elements can be assembled in differing ways. Given this variety, measures that have a fighting chance of delivering reductions in one area may be lost causes in another. The trick is to understand the local problem well enough to direct plausible and potentially cost-effective efforts appropriately at reducing it.

For example, where daytime burglaries take place in households that are empty because their residents are at work, and where those residents are also transitory tenants with no long-term roots in the locality, establishing and maintaining standard Neighbourhood Watches will be an uphill struggle and will be irrelevant to the burglary problem. In some such areas the local forces wished to promote the establishment of traditional Neighbourhood Watches as part of a standard menu of burglary prevention measures, without any apparent thought as to their real relevance to the context of the local burglary problem.

In other cases, the idea behind the proposed project was to try a package in one part of the local authority. If successful, the plan was then to 'roll it out' in the rest of the authority. Such inattention to the specifics of sub-area variations is liable to be very costly. What the suite of evaluations of the Strategic Development Projects are expected to provide are not 'magic bullets' which can be used to reduce burglary anywhere and everywhere. If only we had any! Instead, the aspiration is to produce a series of models showing how interventions fit with local conditions to generate locally cost-effective reductions. The user of the findings, in the wider burglary reduction initiative, will need to adopt measures that have been found to produce falls in saliently similar conditions.

The following section lists most of the interventions that have been included in bids for the SDPs. Many are, of course, well-known already, though some are quite novel. There is much devil in the detail not described here. The following section merely lists types of intervention together with the ways in which they might be expected to reduce the burglary rate. The programme of SDPs as a whole should articulate the potential for specific measures in particular circumstances in more detail and with empirical grounding.

Types of measure

Although many approaches to tackling a local burglary problem were proposed, these can be classified into four generic types that aimed to tackle offender related generators of burglary, victim related generators, specific situational generators and wider locality related generators[5]. Interestingly, there were no measures that aimed to tackle community related generators.

---

[5] See Chapter 2 for a further description of these categories

Offender related measures

Offender related measures were divided into two types – enforcement measures and measures designed to reduce offenders' and potential offenders' propensity for offending. Each of these is described in the following section.

Table 2: *Range of enforcement measures targeted at existing offenders and how they are expected to have their effects*

Measures	How measures are expected to have effects
Eviction of known offenders	Offender removal
Identification of offence series using MOs and contact trace evidence	Risk increase for prolific offenders
Informant targeting	Increased risk to likely offenders; increased uncertainty of offenders; incapacitation of offenders
Market disruption	Difficulty in disposing of stolen goods; reward decrease
Offender targeting	Incapacitation
Stop and search	Increased risk to likely offenders
Trackers for hot products in hot properties	Tracing offenders and receivers leading to incapacitation; risk increase
Use of ASBOs in place of evictions to try to regulate rather than displace known offenders	Avoidance of concentrating likely offenders in privately rented accommodation.

Table 3: *Range of enforcement measures targeted at potential offenders and how they are expected to have their effects*

Measures	How measures are expected to have effects
Are You Sure? Campaigns	Perceived risk increase
Hot spot patrols	Perceived risk increase
Improved clear-up rates	Perceived risk increase
Mobilisation of HIMO landlords	Increased surveillance over offending tenants (for example, dealers in drugs taking stolen goods in exchange)

Given the fact that burglary is a problem for the police and that often the police were the lead agency in producing the SDP bid, it is unsurprising that methods of enforcement featured as a major element in many of the projects we visited. Tables 2 and 3 list the range of enforcement measures being used in SDPs and notes the expected (hypothesised) ways in which these may produce their effects .

The potential efficacy of enforcement in reducing burglary in a particular area clearly depends on various conditions: the degree to which burglary there is committed by a small number of prolific burglars whose high rate persists over a significant period; the identifiability of series of offences and their association with particular offenders or offender groups; the rate at which the courts incarcerate domestic burglars; the rate at which offenders will cease offending at the increased risk of being caught and convicted; the availability of alternative markets for stolen goods if particular methods of disposal are undermined; and so on.

The effectiveness of individual techniques for improvements in enforcement will also depend on the appropriateness of local conditions. For example, tasking informants presumably depends on sufficiently developed networks of offenders and associates to allow information to flow, but not so closed a network that authentic information does not escape to those who can safely pass it on to the police.

A number of SDPs planned to undertake work with known offenders and with those at risk of offending, as outlined in tables 4 and 5. The success of these measures may depend on often complex causal processes linking intervention and outcome (see Ekblom, 1999). For example, drug referral schemes rely on offenders accepting drug treatment, which reduces their demand for drugs, which reduces the need for money, which in turn reduces the need to commit burglary to obtain the money. It was often apparent that interventions were being proposed without being explicit about the processes by which they would be successful and, by implication, without articulating whether the local conditions were suitable for such interventions.

Table 4: Range of treatment measures targeted at existing offenders and how they are expected to have their effects

Measures	How measures are expected to have effects
Drug referral schemes	Demand reduction (proportion of local burglaries associated with drugs problem)
Restorative justice	Conscience increase (some common sense of community membership of victim and offender)
Tailored treatment	Disposition reduction (level of domestic burglars' immersion in groups supporting/justifying burglary)

Treatment measures face difficulties according to local circumstances. They rely in the first instance on apprehending offenders who burgle in the target areas and who are willing to accept treatment. However, in many of the areas we visited clear-up rates were quite low, which meant that referrals to such schemes would be limited unless detections were first increased. Furthermore, insofar as known offenders living in the target area were burgling outside that area, treating these individuals would not reduce the burglary rate there.

Preventive measures aimed at potential offenders face their own difficulties. One problem relates to those measures (such as providing recreational facilities) that aim to target a general population of potential offenders in a target area. By definition, these will be individuals not yet identified as involved in burglary but at risk of offending. The difficulties involved in identifying the appropriate group meant that schemes are often open to all those in a given age range and are thus in effect untargeted.

More focused measures, such as reducing truancy and school exclusion may be more effective at identifying their target group, but necessarily still require 'crystal ball gazing' to determine how many of the group would have committed burglary in the target area if it were not for the intervention.

Table 5: *Range of preventive measures targeted at potential offenders and how they are expected to have their effects*

Measures	**How measures are expected to have effects**
Drugs referral	Demand reduction
Provision of recreational facilities	Increased supervision and decreased supply of likely offenders
Reduced levels of exclusion	Increased supervision and decreased supply of likely offenders
Truancy reduction	Increased supervision and decreased supply of likely offenders

Victim related measures

Tables 6 includes measures that were designed to tackle victim related generators of crime. These focus on changing the behaviour of potential victim groups, thereby reducing their likelihood of burglary victimisation. Cocoon watch helps to reduce the anonymity of neighbours and increases surveillance of neighbouring properties, thereby increasing the risk of detection for the offender. Property marking may help to reduce the demand for stolen goods by a local resident population willing to buy such items. Marked property is likely to be less desirable as it raises awareness of the property's origin and increases the likelihood of being detected handling stolen property. Finally, security awareness campaigns may be beneficial for potential victims unaware of the risk of burglary in their area.

Table 6: *Range of victim related measures and how they are expected to have their effects*

Measures	How measures are expected to have effects
Cocoon watch	Perceived risk increase
Property marking	Perceived reward decrease; risk increase
Security awareness campaigns	Increased caution leading to increased difficulty and risk and reduced reward to offenders

Specific situational measures

Table 7 identifies approaches that tackle specific situational generators of crime. These consist largely of situational crime prevention measures, such as improved security, or improved surveillance. These measures aim to increase the risk of detection, increase the effort required,

Table 7: *Range of specific situational measures and how they are expected to have their effects*

Measures	How measures are expected to have effects
Alarms	(Perceived) risk increase
Alley gating	Effort increase; some risk increase
Bye law for requiring minimum security levels in HIMOs	Security upgrades to population at risk
CCTV	Increased risks
Dwelling target hardening	(Perceived) effort increase
HIMO registration conditions	Security upgrades to population at risk
Household lighting upgrades	Perceived risk increase
Neighbourhood watch	(Perceived) risk increase
Signs of occupancy	Perceived risk and effort increase
University/ college/ agent/ rent guarantor letting conditions	Security upgrades to population at risk
Vacation storage provision	Reduced reward

or reduce the rewards from conducting burglary. Most of the 63 SDPs involved some specific situational measures in their burglary reduction plans.

Wider locality related measures

Wider locality related measures refer to approaches that aim to improve the area in which the burglaries are occurring. This might consist of a whole housing estate, a street, or a group of houses. Table 8 identifies two wider locality related measures that were proposed by partnerships. Both area lighting upgrades and neighbourhood watch schemes aim to increase the risk of detection for the offender by increasing the levels of natural surveillance, either through improved street lighting or by making residents more aware of strangers in the area.

Table 8: *Range of wider locality related measures and how they are expected to have their effects*

Measures	How measures are expected to have effects
Area lighting upgrades	(Perceived) risk increase; community confidence increase
Neighbourhood watch	(Perceived) risk increase

Packages of measures

In almost every case, the SDPs proposed packages of measures. These packages were conceived in different ways. However, it is possible to group these into three kinds – interactive, combined and contradictory packages:

Interactive packages consist of interventions that were designed to work in complementary and cumulative ways. Often there is an important sequencing to the interventions in which the effectiveness of one intervention is dependent on the successful prior implementation of another. A 'crackdown and consolidation' approach provides an example of an interactive package in which an initial police enforcement operation is followed by a programme of community self-confidence building.

Combined packages consist of a range of interventions that work independently of one another. Often these were framed in terms of long lists of interventions without a clear explanation of how they were related or how they combined to form an effective plan for reducing burglary. For example, a number of projects included interventions aimed at offender, potential offender, victim and potential victim.

Contradictory packages consist of interventions that work against each other so that the success of one intervention results in the failure of another. An example of such a package is one containing target hardening and covert detection (such as tracking devices installed in electrical products) in the same properties in which the success of the former is to the detriment of the latter.

The existence of contradictory packages is very telling. It means that many police officers and others think of crime prevention in terms of a tool box, with the assumption that the more numerous the tools, the better. Fundamentally, crime prevention may either attempt to ensure that an offence does not happen, or seek to ensure that it does happen in circumstances wherein its detection is probable or certain. To incorporate elements of both in the same package wastes money. A covert alarm is wasted if the target is adequately hardened. Of course there may be a combination of techniques such that some households are hardened and others are 'baited', but this must be sensitive to the wishes and vulnerabilities of the householders.

Pre-empting burglary

There is no reason to believe that the burglary problem is a constant one. New housing developments present new opportunities. New technology produces new methods for committing burglary, and new means for thwarting it. New building design produces new access challenges and opportunities. New commercial developments, new transport links, and new recreational facilities affect where and when people move and congregate and become aware of crime opportunities. New needs develop, whose satisfaction may motivate burglary. New products susceptible to burglary emerge. New social practices create changed patterns of guardianship and social control. Once and for all solutions to the problem of domestic burglary appear unlikely. Rather, smart burglary reduction calls for routine attention to emerging developments liable to generate fresh offence opportunities and stimuli. The challenge then is to figure out ways of shaping, channeling, modifying, adapting, supplementing, resisting or diverting potentially criminogenic developments, and of exploiting those that potentially inhibit offending.

Current burglary problems result to some degree from an historical lack of foresight. This in turn is presumably a consequence of the fact that no-one with the potential power to act, or to put pressure on others to act, accepted the responsibility to try to anticipate burglary problems and to get something done to pre-empt them. Section 17 of the Crime and Disorder Act (1998) is important in this respect. It assigns responsibility to local authorities, police authorities, National Park authorities, and the Broads Authority to consider and try to prevent the crime and disorder consequences of their policies.

Specific scope for pre-empting burglary problems that have emerged from visits to the SDPs include the following:
- **Designs of new developments:** channelling movement and facilitating natural surveillance. Case one in the Appendix illustrates the crime fall-out from not considering the potential effects of using an estate design that was already producing significant crime problems.

- **Housing allocation methods:** avoiding concentrations of disaffected young males. Again case one shows what can happen if the longer term consequences of housing allocation policies are not considered.
- **In-built security for potential hot products:** two SDP areas are interested in piloting self-locating electronic products. To simplify, these are electronic products which check where they are (through the mains) before permitting themselves to work. This kind of pre-emptive design is an important feature of burglary prevention in the middle and longer term.
- **Siting of crime attractors and generators:** taking account of the criminogenic effects of town planning decisions. The refusal of a local authority to allow a professional football club to move from a town centre to a site on the edge of town (mentioned earlier) is an example of a crime attractor that continues to affect a local community. Housing department allocation policy may also inadvertently generate crime attractors by achieving a critical mass of the criminally inclined.

Several SDPs also included provision for attempts to identify and deal with emerging problems in the local areas covered. In one, a Burglary Analysis Group is dedicated to trying to understand and track problems and to adjust the programme accordingly. This is a step towards looking to developments liable to generate local domestic burglary problems to try and deal with them in advance.

4.   SDPs and the bidding process

In the course of our visits to SDP areas, we got a feel for the bidding process as experienced by those assembling the bids. There are lessons to be learnt both for future rounds of the burglary reduction programme and more generally for programmes in which central government disburses money through a competitive bidding process.

The constraints

Type of area eligible for funding

As already indicated, the requirement that first round SDP project areas comprise 3,000 to 5,000 households with twice the national burglary rate over three years was a considerable technical challenge. Most forces are not well placed easily to scan their areas to identify locations that are eligible in these terms. The boundaries available for aggregating data are normally fixed and do not correspond to the administrative areas of other key agencies (e.g. police beats cannot necessarily be aligned with local authority wards). There are also wide year-on-year fluctuations in burglary rates in many local areas, which make the number of areas with a consistently high burglary problem occasionally difficult to identify. In some cases the areas proposed were not necessarily either 'natural communities' or aggregations of the most burgled geographically grouped households. Both for the second planned set of SDPs and for the roll-out to the remainder of the two million households, there will be benefits either in local areas adopting a more flexible method of drawing boundaries, or Home Office relaxation in the conditions of eligibility for funding.

While burglary risk levels certainly do vary by geography, there may be other dimensions along which risk can be assessed, which may suggest creative approaches for action. We have mentioned examples of 'virtual communities' such as HIMOs and student residents in privately rented housing which have surfaced as potential targets for intervention in the course of looking at potential SDPs.

There may be other categories: known offenders, those moving house and single parent households, for example, seem also to experience high burglary rates. Alternative ways of identifying and targeting constellations of high burglary risk households may be worth pursuing.

Funding available for areas

Bidders for the first tranche of SDPs were informed that they were unlikely to be eligible for more than £60,000 each. There may be benefits in terms both of equity and efficiency in developing a formula for allocating potentially available funds taking account of numbers of households and/or numbers of burglaries, rather than using a simple ceiling. Given that the funding available per project is relatively modest, very radical changes in estate design, very widespread improvements in security levels of individual property, or very elaborate social programmes are unlikely to be feasible or indeed cost-effective. With the sorts of sums of money available, interventions will need to be more subtle or sharply focussed.

Burglary prevention as a self sustaining process

The writers have been exposed to many forward-looking proposals for burglary reduction. This makes one omission all the more conspicuous. Nowhere was there any attempt to generate a self-sustaining process, whereby savings from burglary reduction fed further reduction, creating a benign dynamic. One instance of this might be that a portion of savings which a council makes in reduced burglary costs be explicitly devoted to further burglary reduction. Another might be the use of some of the reduced costs in police time to purchase equipment to facilitate further burglary reduction. Burglary reduction seems to be locked into a sequence of one-off (albeit worthy) projects to address specific problems, with no attempt to generate a benign dynamic of reduction. In one sense, government funding has colluded in this by funding places where the problem is worst. What's in it, in terms of external money and kudos, for areas which have successfully controlled their burglary problem (beyond the substantial but typically uncosted savings)? The next step should surely be the incorporation in proposals of a financial dynamic whereby success in burglary reduction is built upon. Indeed, this will be essential, given the fact that the terms under which funds are allocated from the Crime Reduction Programme stipulate that local partnerships must be committed to continued support for projects, beyond the life of the CRP funding.

Stages in the bidding process
The initial bids

Local areas varied in their familiarity with the processes of preparing bids for government programme funds. The particular emphasis of the SDPs on innovation and well-funded evaluation, as against projects which were concerned with (monitoring) service-delivery, was not appreciated by all. Some of those working in local authorities, which had been eligible to compete for previous government programmes, were old hands at framing their applications. Whilst in some instances this produced bids attuned to the programme aims, in others the SDPs furnished yet another opportunity to wrest (in this case a relatively small sum of) money from central government to deliver or maintain services that mainstream funding could not sustain. Those less experienced in bidding for government funds seemed often to have put more energy into thinking through the substance of their papers, though were sometimes weak in technical presentation.

The provisional target-setting for expected reductions was clearly a problem. In very few cases had realistic targets been set either on the basis of what would be needed to make the initiative cost-effective or on the basis of how the proposed measures might save specific numbers of burglaries. Ideally methods would be chosen which had a realistic chance of producing a fall in the number of burglaries that would make net savings. In practice, we are far from being in a position to do this with much precision with our current understanding of crime prevention. Moreover, the fact that there are good reasons to believe that burglary problems will change means that any such calculation is intrinsically subject to uncertainty. In practice target-setting for reductions in burglary were mostly plucked from the air – roughly small enough to be attainable, but large enough to satisfy the Home Office.

The development visits

Those visited were not always fully clear what was expected of them. In some cases, nothing had been done further to develop the outline bid since its initial submission. Here, the development visit was treated as the occasion to work through what might in practice be implemented. Moreover, it was not uncommon to attend meetings with people who had not previously met one another but were identified as partners in the proposed initiative. In other cases, local groups had undertaken substantial further research and development work and had a set of quite detailed ideas about what they might do, and how it might impact on the local burglary problem. In most cases, more could be achieved where some follow-up work had been done. Where very little was known about the local problem, and a standard set of conventional recipe responses had been proposed or where there were just vague aspirations, it was more difficult to engage in constructive dialogue with those seen.

In a few visits, though those seen were almost always courteous and hospitable, there was some incredulity that proposals were being probed, and suggestions made that there may be benefits in some rethinking. It would appear that some other programmes require applicants to jump through far fewer hoops for much larger sums of money.

It was invariably useful to visit the site of the proposed initiative and to talk about the area and its burglary problem with those who had first hand experience of working in the area. Beat officers, some crime prevention officers, and some local housing officers, where they had spent a significant time attached to the target areas, were especially informative. It is likely that they have a very useful role in helping shape proposals. They had been underused in some areas.

The revised bids

In some cases the revised bids included much more detailed costed plans and explanations for them than were required in the original outline bids. They showed that there had been a substantial re-think in the light of discussions during the development day and further analysis of locally available data. In other cases, there appears to have been little further thought. In one or two cases there had been a great deal of further analysis making better sense of the local problem but little adjustment to the strategy in the light of that work.

Much was achieved in a relatively short period of time. Over a six month period, a programme was devised, a bidding prospectus issued, bids received, short-listed and visited, costed plans were produced and projects were launched. In the rush to launch the initiative, a number of aspects were overlooked, or not dealt with as efficiently as they might otherwise have been. However, we now have the opportunity to incorporate the lessons we have learned in to future rounds of the initiative.

5.   Conclusions and Recommendations

The SDP development visits provided a valuable insight into the range of burglary problems that currently exist in England and Wales and the variety of approaches taken to address those problems.

The following section offers recommendations on how burglary reduction efforts might be improved. There are issues of relevance to those planning burglary reduction projects at the local level, as well as how programmes of this kind are organised centrally. A number of recommendations are also made for ways in which burglary might be reduced through intervention at the national level.

Issues for those planning efforts to reduce burglary locally

1. Taking a strategic perspective: It is helpful to consider burglary reduction projects from a strategic standpoint that involves identifying and analysing the problem, devising solutions, assessing the likely impact of solutions, reviewing progress, refining approaches and evaluating success. In this regard, existing management tools, such as the 'SARA' process that involves Scanning, Analysis, Response and Assessment (see Leigh et al. 1996) may prove useful.

2. Assembling the local team: In each local area, there is a range of personnel with different skills, experiences and knowledge that may be drawn on to assist in devising burglary solutions. For example, crime analysts may be able to bring skills in identifying more precisely the nature and extent of the burglary problem. This could be supplemented by drawing on the local knowledge of beat officers, local authority housing department staff, local residents and so on. While there is no reason why single-agency strategies for reducing burglary cannot achieve success, the chances are much higher if the strategy involves joint working. Key agencies in a comprehensive burglary reduction strategy may include the probation service, the local authority, housing, planning and regeneration departments and the health authority as well as the police.

3. Checking data: Analysis of available data will be important in defining the problem. It is essential that information is double-checked before it is acted upon, to avoid misallocating resources later.

4. Testing assumptions: At the local level, there will often be assumptions, or common held beliefs about the nature of the burglary problem and its causes. It is important that assumptions are tested with available information and to distinguish between approaches that are founded on 'facts' and those based on unsubstantiated beliefs. The data analysis upon which assumptions are tested will require access to IT systems holding relevant information, software for analysing the information and a competent analyst with the skills to interrogate data.

5. Devising suitable crime reduction plans: In developing the local burglary reduction plan, it is important to ensure that the component parts of the strategy complement each other. Each element of the plan should be scrutinised in terms of the additional benefit it will bring in burglary reduction and to ensure it does not inhibit the effectiveness of other aspects of the strategy. Plans should also be developed with a view to long term sustainability of interventions, rather than concentrating on short-term reductions. Furthermore, they should be properly integrated with the local Crime and Disorder strategies.

6. Creating a self-sustaining process: Burglary reduction strategies should, ideally, incorporate plans to reinvest some of the savings from successful schemes, thereby creating a process that will continue to tackle burglary in the longer term.

7. Adjust priorities to reflect crime reduction needs: Many local authority decisions are likely to have a potential impact on the local crime problem. For example, the phasing of improvements to social housing, or the upgrading of street lighting could have an impact on the distribution of crime at the local level.

For the future operation of the burglary reduction initiative

8. Allowing time for preparation of plans: The first phase of the burglary reduction initiative was launched within a tight timescale. There may be merit in allowing local Crime and Disorder Partnerships more time to analyse their problem and develop suitable plans.

9. Clarify offence categories covered by initiative: To avoid further confusion, future guidance should specify more clearly the types of burglary that will be eligible for funding.

10. Allow plans to tackle 'virtual communities': The first phase of the burglary reduction initiative focused on area based problems. However, there would appear to be a number of burglary problems that are not best suited to geographical analysis, such as victimisation of students and those residing in houses of multiple occupation. To maximise the potential of the initiative, these types of community should be included within the funding criteria for future phases of the programme.

11. Adjust funding formula: The first round of the initiative offered a fixed ceiling for each area, which took no account of the size of the area or the extent of burglary victimisation. Future funding rounds would benefit from a sliding scale of funding, based on the number of households, or number of burglaries suffered.

Issues that might be addressed centrally to reduce burglary

12. Local authorities should consider crime pattern consequences in adjudicating planning applications: Burglary problems can be generated by planning decisions that have unforseen negative consequences. Similarly, it is possible to alleviate burglary problems by accepting planning applications, if that application involves moving a crime generator (such as a football stadium) away from a highly victimised area. Section 17 of the Crime and Disorder Act may well provide the necessary mechanism by which local authorities are, in future, held to account for planning decisions that impact on crime.

13. Committee of Vice Chancellors and Principals (CVCP) should consider what they might do collectively to reduce the vulnerability of students to burglary: Students fulfil many of the criteria associated with high burglary victimisation. While this can be tackled at the local area, there would also be benefits in targeting this group direct through the CVCP. Possible measures include the provision of crime prevention advice to 'freshers' and access to secure storage space during vacations.

14. Encourage manufacturers to identify 'hot products' and engage in pre-emptive design to reduce their desirability. The fact that burglary often involves the theft of a limited range of electronic products (televisions, videos hi-fis computers etc.) suggests that there is the potential for designing crime prevention features into these items (Clarke, 1999). This is the subject of another strand of the Crime Reduction Programme that focuses on national initiatives for reducing crime.

15. Promote campaigns that reduce the acceptability of buying stolen goods. Burglary can only be sustained as long as there are people willing to buy stolen goods – knowingly or otherwise. Publicity campaigns, allied with higher profile enforcement, may help to reduce the desirability of buying stolen goods, thereby reducing the returns for the burglary offender (Kock et al., 1996; Sutton, 1998).

Concluding remarks

The first phase of the burglary reduction initiative has revealed a great deal about the burglary problem and has highlighted the fact that there is much work to be done if burglary is to be reduced nationally. The partnerships we visited had worked hard to devise sensible, evidence based approaches to burglary prevention that were tailored to their local problem. This is a model that we will need to refine for future stages of the programme, to ensure that the solutions proposed are the most cost effective and efficient available for tackling burglary.

Anderson, D, Chenery, S, and K. Pease (1995) *Biting Back: Tackling Repeat Burglary and Car Crime*, Crime Prevention and Detection Series Paper 58, London: Home Office.

Bennett, T. and R. Wright (1984) *Burglars on Burglary*, Farnborough, Hants: Gower.

Chenery, S, Holt, J, and K. Pease (1997) *Biting Back II: Reducing Repeat Victimisation in Huddersfield*, Crime Prevention and Detection Series Paper 58, London: Home Office.

Clarke, R.V. (1999) *Hot Products: Understanding, Anticipating, and Reducing Demand for Stolen Goods*, Crime Prevention and Detection Series Paper 112, London: Home Office.

Davidson, N. (1984) *Burglary in the Community: Patterns of Localisation in Offender Victim Relations*, in R. Clarke and T. Hope (eds) Coping with Burglary: Research Perspectives on Policy, Boston: Kleuer Nijhoff.

Ekblom, P., Law, H. and M. Sutton (1996) *Safer Cities and Domestic Burglary*, Home Office Research Study 164, London: Home Office.

Ekblom, P. (1999) *The Conjunction of Criminal Opportunities - A tool for clear, joined-up thinking about community safety and crime prevention*. In V. McLaren et al (ed) Key Issues in Crime Prevention and Community Safety. London: IPPR

Farrell, G. and K. Pease (1993) *Once Bitten, Twice Bitten*, Crime Prevention Unit Paper 46, London, Home Office.

Forrester, D., Chatterton, M. and K. Pease (1998) *The Kirkholt Burglary Prevention Project*, Rochdale, Crime Prevention Unit Paper 13, London, Home Office.

Forrester, D., Frenz, S., O'Connell, M. and K. Pease (1990) *The Kirkholt Burglary Prevention Project, Phase 11*, Crime Prevention Unit Paper 23, London, Home Office

Felson, M. (1998) *Crime and Everyday Life*, 2nd Edition, Thousand Oaks, CA: Pine Forge Press.

Garfinkel, H. (1967) *Studies in Ethnomethodology*, Englewood Cliffs, NJ: Prentice-Hall

Goldblatt, P. and Lewis, C. (1998) *Reducing Offending: an Assessment of Research Evidence on Ways of Dealing with Offending Behaviour*, Home Office Research Study 187, London: Home Office.

Kock, E., Kemp, T. and Rix, B (1996) *Disrupting the Distribution of Stolen Electrical Goods* Crime Prevention and Detection Series Paper 69, London: Home Office.

Laycock, G. (1992) *Operation Identification, or the Power of Publicitry*, in R. Clarke (ed) Situational Crime Prevention: Successful Case Studies, New York: Harrow and Heston.

Leigh, A., Read, T. and Tilley, N. (1996) *Problem-Oriented Policing: Brit Pop*, Crime Prevention and Detection Series Paper 75, London: Home Office.

Mirrlees-Black, C., Budd, T., Partridge, S. and P. Mayhew (1998) *The 1998 British Crime Survey*, London: Home Office

Pease, K. (1992) *Preventing Burglary on a British Housing Estate*, in R. Clarke (ed) Situational Crime Prevention: Successful Case Studies, New York: Harrow and Heston.

Polvi, N., Looman, T, Humphries, C., and K. Pease (1990) *Repeat Break and Enter Victimisation: Time Course and Crime Prevention Opportunity*, Journal of Police Science and Administration, Vol 17, 8-11.

Reiss, A.J. (1988) *Co-offending and Criminal Careers* in Tonry, M. and Morris, N. (ed) Crime and Justice: A Review of Research. Vol. 10. Chicago: University of Chicago Press

Reiss, A.J. and Farrington, D.P. (1991) *Advancing Knowledge about Co-offending: Results from a Prospective Longitudinal Survey of London Males* Journal of Criminal Law and Criminology. Vol 82 (2) pp. 360-395

Stockdale, J and P. Gresham (1995) *Combating Burglary: An Evaluation of Three Strategies*, Crime Prevention and Detection Series Paper 59, London: Home Office.

Sutton, M. (1998) *Handling Stolen Goods and Theft: A Market Reduction Approach*, Home Office Research Study 178, London: Home Office.

Tilley, N. and J. Webb (1994) *Burglary Reduction: Findings from Safer Cities Schemes*, Crime Prevention Unit Paper 51, London, Home Office

Winchester, S. and H. Jackson (1982) *Residential Burglary: the Limits of Prevention*, Home Office Research Study 74, London: Home Office.

Appendix

Key generators of high burglary rates – examples drawn from development visits

Case one: *Combining defective housing design with defective housing allocation policy*

This is an 11 year old estate, which has quickly deteriorated, and is now in poor condition. Domestic burglary is one serious problem among many. The estate has a very unkempt appearance. There are abandoned and burned out cars, many broken fences, piles of dumped waste, widespread graffiti, and a lot of overgrown waste ground.

Housing allocation policies and practices seem to have interacted with design features of the estate to provoke a spiral of physical and social decline:

1. The houses are small, and have been allocated primarily to single parents.
2. Men fathering the children are often not part of the household but are occasional visitors.
3. There is a shortage of adequate male role models. (There was even a hint that some of the older men visiting the estate may recruit youngsters into crime)
4. Parental supervision tends to be weak.
5. The alleyways, disorganised open space and shortage of recreational facilities provide conditions in which young people have limited opportunities for constructive use of their leisure time and wide opportunities to misbehave.
6. The poor physical conditions that result from vandalism and neglect reduce the attractiveness of the area to new tenants and dispose those with the resources to do so to leave.
7. There are thus many boarded up voids, adding to the unattractive appearance of the estate.
8. These boarded up properties reduce ambient light levels at night since they are not making their normal contribution. Poor lighting levels contribute to the dingy atmosphere and reduce scope for natural surveillance.
9. Because the housing is unpopular, it attracts only tenants who are disorganised and/or desperate.
10. Available housing is allocated to single parents in difficulty.

And so the spiral continues.

It was suggested that prevailing family patterns and the absence of resources or opportunities for entertainment outside the home meant that houses had good supplies of attractive goods for burglars: portable, high value, readily saleable videos, televisions, CD disks and players, computer games, and so on. Moreover the poverty of community members made them likely customers for stolen goods, which are sold door to door. It was noted also that many residents were unable to obtain insurance, further fuelling interest in replacing stolen goods cheaply.

The age of the estate is also deemed significant. The children of the cohort of single parents originally allocated the housing are reaching their teens. They are coming to the peak age for offending.

In this case, the key generators of burglary are:

- a good supply of attractive goods for theft
- a growing supply of likely offenders
- limited capacity for surveillance and social control
- a potential market for stolen property.

Case two: Mixing the old and the new - Victorian terraces occupied by students

The target area is adjacent to the town centre of a university town. The area is bisected by a major shopping street leading into the city centre, which evidently draws in large numbers at night-times.

The university sits at the heart of the area. Students comprise a significant proportion of the resident population, especially in term time. Analysis of the crime report data revealed that 173 (19%) of the victims were identified as students, though, because the crime report field relating to victim occupation was not completed reliably, this represents a minimum. There was a marked seasonal pattern to the burglaries known to be committed against students. From May to September there was an average of less than five burglaries per month. For the remaining months (October to April) the average was 19, with the four months January to April each recording 25 or more burglaries. Students are deemed to be at especially high risk because of their possession of attractive electrical goods, the insecurity of their rented accommodation, and their lack of awareness of the need to take precautions.

With few exceptions the houses are small, two storey terraced dwellings built in the early years of the century. In almost all cases a wide, dog-leg alleyway runs between the backs of the terraces. Most are evidently poorly lit, and are typically strewn with rubbish. There are small walled yards to the rear of each house. The walls are about six to seven feet high in most cases. Quite a large number of the houses have single storey flat roof extensions running to the yard's back wall. The extension roof was generally roughly the same height as the wall. In many cases, broken glass had been cemented into the top of the rear walls to discourage burglars from climbing over. Almost all burglaries, where direction of entry was recorded, were from the back.

In addition to the small terraced houses there are some larger houses, the majority of which are found in just two streets. Many of these are now small hotels providing accommodation for a transient population. Some residents are paid for by DSS and a proportion have been displaced from estates, where they have been evicted, often because of anti-social behaviour.

The area has quite a high known-offender resident population (233 individuals in all) and is frequented by still more (655 and 544 in each of two wards, including their resident known-offenders).

Here, the key generators of burglary are:

- a victim group (students) that is not particularly security conscious
- a good supply of attractive goods for theft (students' electrical goods)
- a supply of likely offenders living in the area
- housing design with limited capacity for surveillance at rear

Case three: Mixed housing with mixed offender populations

There are three main residential areas in this ward. Area One comprises a 1960s council estate with a Radburn lay-out, coupled with some privately owned Victorian terraced housing. Area Two is an inter-war council estate. Area Three is made up of recently built privately owned and housing association dwellings. Further housing is being built on this estate.

Much of the burglary (and other crime) problem in Area Three was attributed to the residents of a small neighbouring estate. It was striking that over 20 houses next to the estate were boarded up. Residents had evidently suffered so much crime and harassment that they had moved out. Having initially been sold for about £65,000 in 1995, the houses are now worth only £20,000. New houses, however, are still being built next to those boarded up.

Much of the Area Two problem was attributed to the established local offenders, who are concentrated in one area. There is evidently a culture of non co-operation with the police and serious intimidation of those who 'grass'.

Burglary in Area One was associated with the Radburn lay-out. An extensive programme of building high walls cutting off escape routes and channelling movement is currently under way. Crime problems were also attributed to residents of a hostel for 16 to 25 year olds, who evidently quickly develop offending relationships with other youngsters in the area. The local beat officer suggested that this hostel is a conduit through which new offending techniques are learned.

In this target area, the key generators of burglary varied in different parts of it. They include:

- resident/nearby offending populations
- ineffective informal social control, and significant witness intimidation
- some poor building/estate design limiting scope for surveillance
- a process of differential association through an informal network of young offenders.

Case four: The 'honey-pot' effect

This project covers a small, mainly residential area dominated by student rentals in small privately rented terraced housing. Burglary rates are currently around 150 per 1,000 households, among the highest in the city. (The beat accounts for just over 1% of the total population in the sub-division, but 7% of its burglaries.) Clear-up rates are very low (6/155 in 1998).

Offenders are drawn into the area from outside and target the area as having poor security, poor guardianship and rich pickings. Over half the victims are students, known to be a population that is relatively well endowed with desirable electrical products. The area has much in common with Case 2, including highly similar housing stock. However in contrast to Case 2, which had a rich supply of indigenous offenders, offenders were thought by the police to be drawn from elsewhere into the area (like bees to a honey-pot).

The key generators of burglary in this area were:

- A population of tenants, initially naïve about crime risks, unprepared or unable to invest in security
- A transient population, replaced on an annual basis, with little investment in the area
- Poor quality housing stock with little physical security
- Absentee landlords with no particular incentive to upgrade security
- A visiting population of offenders willing to travel into the area in order to commit crime

Case five: The twilight world of bed-sit land

This area is in a striving holiday town with a population of 30,000. The town has clearly fallen on hard times, having lost its position as a popular resort, and found no significant replacement to holiday trade. Unemployment is high at around 20%. The target area is dominated by hotels and bed and breakfast establishments, now converted to housing in multiple occupation (HIMOs) and rented out to people on unemployment and housing benefit. The area seems to be in steep decline. Even the student population, with which the area used to be popular, has moved out.

Burglary problems are roughly twice the national average in the target area, and are focussed on HIMOs. On the basis of known offenders (and the burglary clear up rate here is around 11%) the majority of offenders are in their late teens or early twenties. Common targets are furniture, light electrical goods, and jewellery. Offenders are thought to be non-specialists, 'surfing' between different sorts of crime. Stolen goods are thought to be disposed of through integrated networks, and are often stolen to order. Outlets for stolen goods include second-hand shops (of which there are several) and off-licenses. Drug use is likely to be a feature of some burglars' offending.

In this area, the key generators of crime are considered to be:

- a transient population, living in relative anonymity, reducing the potential for effective natural surveillance
- a supply of HIMOs, that commonly consist of shared hallways and corridors where it is not unusual to see strangers
- housing provision that attracts socio-economic groups most at risk of engaging in burglary
- a local drug culture that may fuel property crime in the area

Related RDS Publications

Burglary of Domestic Dwellings: Findings from the British Crime Survey. Budd, T. (1999) Home Office Statistical Bulletin 4/99. London: Home Office

Preventing Residential Burglary in Cambridge: From Crime Audits to Targeted Strategies. Bennett, T. and Durie, L. (1999) Police Research Series, Paper 108. London: Home Office

Auditing Crime and Disorder: Guidance for local pertnerships. Hough, M. and Tilley, N. (1998) Crime Detection and Prevention Series. Paper 91. London: Home Office

Getting the Grease to the Squeak: Research Lessons for Crime Prevention. Hough, M. and Tilley, N. (1998) Crime Detection and Prevention Series, Paper 85. London: Home Office

Repeat Vicitmisation: Taking Stock. Pease, K (1998) Crime Detection and Prevention Series, Paper 90. London: Home Office

Biting Back II: Reducing Repeat Vicitmisation in Huddersfield. Chenery, S., Holt, J. and Pease, K. (1997) Crime Detection and Prevention Series, Paper 82. London: Home Office

Biting Back: Tackling Repeat Burglary and Car Crime. Anderson, D., Chenery, S. and Pease, K. (1995) Crime Detection and Prevention Series, Paper 58. London: Home Office

Safer Cities and Domestic Burglary. Ekblom, P., Law, H. and Sutton, M. (1996) Home Office Research Study 164. London: Home Office

The PRG Burglary Manual. Bridgeman, C. and Taylor-Browne, J. (1996) London: Home Office

Combating Burglary: An Evaluation of Three Strategies. Stockdale, J., and Gresham, P. (1995) Crime Detection and Prevention Series, Paper 59. London: Home Office

Targeted Crime Reduction for Local Areas: Principles and Methods. Shapland, J., Wiles, P. and Wilcox, P. (1994) London: Home Office

Policing & Reducing Crime Unit
Research, Development & Statistics Directorate
Home Office
Clive House, London SW1H 9HD

Tel: 020 7271 8225 Fax: 020 7271 8344

www.homeoffice.gov.uk/prghome.htm